Exquisite Seafood Pasta Sauce for Any Occasion

30 Recipes That Will Have You Reaching for Seconds

BY

Carla Hale

License Notes

No part of this Book can be reproduced in any form or by any means including print, electronic, scanning or photocopying unless prior permission is granted by the author.

All ideas, suggestions and guidelines mentioned here are written for informative purposes. While the author has taken every possible step to ensure accuracy, all readers are advised to follow information at their own risk. The author cannot be held responsible for personal and/or commercial damages in case of misinterpreting and misunderstanding any part of this Book

Table of Contents

Introduction

Are you a seafood lover and a pasta lover? Have you been searching for unique and delicious recipes that will combine your two culinary passions?

Then this seafood pasta sauce book is just what you have been looking for! With this cookbook, you will learn how to make mouth-watering recipes with simple ingredients and less than 20 minutes of preparation time. With such delicacies as shrimp, scallops, lobster and tuna, you will be well on your way to creating culinary masterpieces that the family will devour.

No longer will pasta be dull and lifeless, the same tomato-based sauces being re-used over and over. With these 30 sauce recipes, you will turn your dinner table into a banquet fit for the King of the Sea.

Smoked Salmon Alfredo Sauce

This alfredo sauce is creamy and delectable when tossed with some tender linguine and serve with a chilled glass of wine. The flavor of the smoked salmon is addictive from the first bite.

Preparation Time:10 minutes

Servings:4

Ingredients:

- 1/4 chopped onion
- 2 ounces butter
- 8 ounces chopped smoked salmon, chopped
- 16 ounces heavy whipping cream
- 1 diced tomato
- 1 ounce fresh parsley, chopped
- a pinch of black pepper, ground

Directions:

1. Melt butter in a frying pan on medium heat. Add onion to the butter and sauté until translucent.

2. Sauté salmon with the onion for 2 minutes

3. Gradually add cream to the pan and stir until thickened.

4. Top cream with tomato and parsley

Smoked Salmon and Vodka Cream Sauce

This creamy sauce tastes amazing poured over some spaghetti with chives and black pepper. Even though the heavy whipping cream is a few extra calories, the creamy texture is well worth it.

Preparation Time:20 minutes

Servings:2

Ingredients:

- ½ ounce butter
- 1/2 ounce onion, finely diced
- 4 ounces smoked salmon, diced
- 2 fluid ounces vodka
- 2 ounces heavy whipping cream
- 2 ounces tomatoes, chopped
- 4 ounces tomato sauce
- a pinch of salt
- a pinch of black pepper, ground
- a pinch nutmeg, ground
- 1/8 tablespoon cayenne pepper

Directions:

1. Melt butter in a saucepan. Add onion and smoked salmon to the butter and sauté.

2. When the pan starts to smoke, remove from heat and pour in vodka.

3. Return sauce to the heat when the vodka burns off and add tomatoes, tomato sauce and cream to the pan. Mix well.

4. Season with the remaining ingredients and cook until sauce has reached desired thickness.

Puttanesca

I love the salty flavor of the anchovies in this simple puttanesca recipe. Match that with the olives and capers and you have one delicious sauce that tastes amazing with a fruity glass of wine

Preparation Time:5 minutes

Servings:4

Ingredients:

- 2 ½ ounces olive oil
- 3 minced cloves garlic
- 1/4 teaspoon crushed red pepper flakes
- 1 teaspoon oregano, dried
- 3 chopped anchovy fillets
- 30 ounces canned diced tomatoes, drained.
- 8 ounces spaghetti
- 4 ounces pitted kalamata olives, chopped
- 2 ounces chopped capers

Directions:

1. Bring a large pot of lightly salted water to a boil on high heat.

2. Pour oil into a cold frying pan and add garlic to the oil. Increase heat to medium low and stir garlic until fragrant for 2 minutes

3. Add pepper flakes, oregano and anchovies to the garlic and cook for 2 minutes until anchovies break apart.

4. Add tomatoes to the frying pan, increase heat to medium high and bring mixture to a simmer.

5. Crush tomatoes with the back of a spoon as you cook. Simmer mixture for 10 minutes until liquid is reduced

6. Cook pasta in boiling water for 9 minutes until al dente

7. Reserve 4 ounces of pasta water.

8. Add olives and capers to the sauce and stir well. Toss sauce with pasta in the pot for 1 minute until pasta is cooked. Add reserved pasta water if the puttanesca is too thick

Pink Shrimp Sauce

The shrimp in this sauce is plump, juicy and will have your taste buds singing. Serve this shrimp sauce with some white rice or your favorite pasta.

Preparation Time:5 minutes

Servings:4

Ingredients:

- 2 ounces tomato puree
- 6 ounces water
- 8 ounces heavy cream
- 1/4 ounce fresh ginger root, grated
- 1/4 teaspoon cayenne pepper
- 2/3 ounce lemon juice
- 1 teaspoon cumin, ground
- 1 teaspoon salt
- a pinch of ground black pepper
- 1/2 teaspoon white sugar
- 1 ½ ounces vegetable oil
- 1/2 ounce mustard seed
- 2 chopped cloves garlic
- 32 ounces peeled medium shrimp, deveined
- a pinch of salt
- a pinch of ground black pepper

Directions:

1. Put puree in a measuring cup and add enough water to fill 8 ounces. Pour into a bowl.

2. Add cream, ginger, cayenne, lemon juice, cumin,1 teaspoon of salt, pepper and sugar to the bowl and mix until combined. Chill for 1 hour

3. Heat oil in a skillet on medium high heat. Cook mustard seeds in the oil until they start to pop. Add garlic right away and stir once.

4. Add shrimp to the skillet and stir until opaque. Season with salt and pepper.

5. Add pink sauce to the skillet and stir until sauce is bubbling.

White Clam Sauce

This sauce is so decadent and delicious, your guests will think you smuggled it in from a gourmet shop. I love serving this dish over some linguine with grated parmesan.

Preparation Time: 5 minutes

Servings: 4

Ingredients:

- 4 ounces olive oil
- 1 large chopped onion
- 6 minced cloves garlic
- a pinch red pepper flakes
- 14 ounces half-and-half cream
- 19 ½ ounces canned minced clams, drained and reserved juice

Directions:

1. Heat oil in a large frying pan on medium high heat.

2. Sauté onion and pepper flakes in the oil. Stir until onion is tender. Then add garlic and cook for 2 minutes until fragrant.

3. Pour the clam juice and cook for 10 minutes.

4. Slowly add cream to the skillet and stir. Cook for 20 minutes, but do not bring to a boil.

5. Cook linguine pasta according to the instructions on the package.

6. Add clams to the sauce in the frying pan until heated through.

7. Remove pan from heat and serve.

Cajun Sauce

This sauce is as delicious and creamy as any meal you would buy at a Cajun food restaurant. Try serving this with a glass of the same wine you used for cooking

Preparation Time:10 minutes

Servings:2

Ingredients:

- 2 ounces butter
- 8 sliced fresh mushrooms,
- 8 peeled medium shrimp, deveined
- 2 ounces whipping cream
- a pinch of garlic powder
- a pinch black pepper
- 1/3 ounce Madeira wine

Directions:

1. Melt 1 teaspoon of butter in a saucepan. Sauté mushrooms in the butter until tender. Add shrimp to the pan and cook until translucent. Transfer mixture from the pan to a bowl.

2. Melt the rest of the butter in the same saucepan. Gradually add cream and stir in shrimp and mushroom. Season with garlic and pepper and simmer until thickened.

3. Stir in wine just before serving

Lobster Mornay Sauce

This lobster sauce will have everyone reaching for seconds when served with some tender pasta and garlic bread. I like to reserve some mushrooms so I can garnish the servings with a few slices.

Preparation Time: 10 minutes

Servings: 4

Ingredients:

- 2 ounces butter
- 8 ounces fresh mushrooms, sliced
- 16 ounces diced lobster meat
- 2 ounces all-purpose flour
- 8 ounces chicken broth
- 8 ounces heavy cream
- 1/2 teaspoon pepper
- 4 ounces Parmesan cheese, freshly grated

Directions:

1. Melt butter in a pan on medium heat. Add mushrooms and gently stir until tender.

2. Add lobster meat to the mixture in the pan and cook until opaque.

3. Remove the mushrooms and the lobster meat from the pan and set aside.

4. Reduce heat to low and sprinkle flour in the same pan. Cook for 2 minutes, add chicken broth, heavy cream and pepper and stir well. Simmer for 10 minutes until it reaches desired thickness.

5. Add mushrooms, lobster and parmesan to the sauce and stir well. Cook for 5 minutes before serving.

Sauce with Shrimp and Scallops

Be careful not to overcook the shrimp and scallops as they tend to get tough if cooked for too long. The best rule of thumb is to remove them just before the shrimp turn completely pink and replace back into the sauce five minutes before serving.

Preparation Time:20 minutes

Servings:8

Ingredients:

- 2 ounces olive oil, divided
- 6 crushed cloves garlic
- 24 ounces whole tomatoes with liquid, peeled and chopped
- 1/4 ounce salt
- 1 teaspoon crushed red pepper flakes
- 16 ounces package linguine pasta
- 8 ounces small peeled shrimp, deveined
- 8 ounces bay scallops
- 1/2 ounce fresh parsley, chopped

Directions:

1. Heat 1 ounce of oil in a large saucepan. Add garlic to the oil and sauté until fragrant. Pour tomatoes into the pan and season with salt and pepper flakes. Bring mixture to a boil.

2. Reduce heat and simmer mixture for 30 minutes. Stir occasionally.

3. Cook pasta according to the package instructions. Drain.

4. Heat 1 ounce of olive oil in a frying pan on high heat. Add shrimp and scallops to the oil and cook for 2 minutes. Stir frequently until the shrimp turns opaque.

5. Stir shrimp and scallops with the tomato mixture and add parsley. Stir well and cook for 4 minutes until the sauce begins to bubble.

Tuna and Tomato Pasta Sauce

This simple tuna and tomato sauce recipe tastes wonderful over a bed of spaghetti with some grated parmesan. I like to serve this pasta sauce with a sprig of fresh parsley for garnish.

Preparation Time: 15 minutes

Servings: 2

Ingredients:

- 1 ½ ounces olive oil
- 1 medium chopped onion
- 2 Chopped garlic cloves
- 8 ounces canned tomato with juice
- 1/4 teaspoon dried oregano
- A pinch of salt and black pepper
- 1 drained can of flaked tuna
- 1 ounce green olives, sliced with a small amount of juice reserved
- ½ ounce capers, with a small amount of juice reserved

Directions:

1. Heat oil in a saucepan on medium heat. Sauté onion and garlic in the oil until tender and fragrant, about 5 minutes.

2. Stir in tomatoes, oregano, salt and pepper and reduce heat to low. Simmer for 10 minutes until heated through.

3. Add the rest of the ingredients and cook for 5-10 minutes more until sauce reaches desired thickness.

Puttanesca II

Here is another puttanesca recipe that will have your mouth watering. Serve this delectable sauce over a bed of pappardelle pasta with a glass of white wine.

Preparation Time:20 minutes

Servings:8

Ingredients:

- 2 ounces extra-virgin olive oil
- 16 ounces mushrooms, sliced
- 1 ounce minced garlic
- 8 ounces dry white wine
- 5 ounce drained jar of anchovy-stuffed green olives, halved
- 2 ounces drained capers
- 1 ounce caper juice
- 28 ounces canned crushed tomatoes
- a pinch red pepper flakes

Directions:

1. Heat oil in a large frying pan on medium high heat. Add mushrooms and garlic to the oil and cook for 4 minutes until mushrooms brown.

2. Increase heat to high and add wine. Bring mixture to a boil and stir in olives, capers and juice, tomatoes and pepper flakes.

3. Reduce heat again and simmer on medium low for 20 minutes

Marinara with White Wine Sauce

The anchovies add a salty addictive flavor to this superb sauce recipe. I love serving this sauce over a bed of spaghetti with some freshly grated parmesan and a pinch of basil.

Preparation Time: 25 minutes

Servings: 10

Ingredients:

- ½ ounce olive oil from anchovies
- 1 ounce garlic, minced
- 4 ounces onion, chopped
- 1 chopped green bell pepper
- 4 ounces white wine
- 24 ounces grape tomatoes
- 15 ounces canned stewed tomatoes, with juice
- 6 anchovy fillets
- 1/2 teaspoon salt
- a pinch of black pepper
- 1/2 teaspoon basil, dried
- 1 teaspoon parsley, chopped
- 1/2 teaspoon oregano, dried
- 1 small bay leaf

Directions:

1. Heat anchovy oil in a pan on medium heat. Add garlic, onions and bell pepper to the oil. Stir until onion turns translucent.

2. Pour wine into the pan and simmer until liquid is reduced by half.

3. Place grape and stewed tomatoes in a food processor with anchovies and puree until smooth. Add the rest of the ingredients to the puree and pour into the pot.

4. Bring sauce to a simmer on medium high heat and cook for 1 hour.

The Best White Clam Sauce

The canned clams are the easiest to use in this recipe, but you can also use fresh and mince them yourself. I love this sauce with linguine and garlic bed served with my favorite Chardonnay.

Preparation Time:5 minutes

Servings:4

Ingredients:

- 4 ounces olive oil
- 1 large chopped onion
- 6 minced cloves garlic
- a pinch red pepper flakes
- 14 ounces half-and-half cream
- 19 ½ ounces canned minced clams, drained with juice reserved
- 2 ounces Parmesan cheese, grated
- 8 ounces dried linguine pasta

Directions:

1. Heat oil in a large frying pan on medium high heat.

2. Add onion and pepper flakes to the oil and cook until onion is translucent. Stir constantly.

3. Stir in garlic and cook for 2 minutes until fragrant.

4. Pour in clam juice and simmer for 10 minutes.

5. Slowly stir cream into the frying pan and simmer for 20 minutes. Do not boil.

6. Cook linguine according to the package instructions.

7. Stir in clams to the sauce and cook until heated through. Toss sauce with pasta and serve topped with parmesan cheese.

Crab Cake Sauce

Try this delicious sauce with your favorite crab cake recipe
the next time you bake. The lemon and yogurt create a tangy
and refreshing flavor you will love.

Preparation Time:5 minutes

Servings:12

Ingredients:

- 8 ounces sour cream
- 8 ounces mayonnaise
- 4 ounces cottage cheese
- 2 ½ ounces hot salsa
- 1/4 teaspoon cayenne pepper
- 1/2 ounce lemon juice
- 14 ounces plain yogurt

Directions:

1. Combine all ingredients in a blender and puree until smooth. Chill for 1 hour before serving

Mussels in Curry Cream Sauce

The mussels are tasty and tender in this creamy curry sauce.
I usually serve this over a bed of Rotini noodles with a glass
of white wine.

Preparation Time:40 minutes

Servings:4

Ingredients:

- 4 ounces shallots, minced
- 1 ounce garlic, minced
- 12 ounces dry white wine
- 8 ounces heavy cream
- 1 teaspoon curry powder
- 32 cleaned and debearded mussels
- 2 ounces butter
- 2 ounces parsley, minced
- 2 ounces green onions, chopped

Directions:

1. Bring wine to a simmer in a large pan. Cook shallots and garlic in the wine until translucent.

2. Add cream and curry powder to the pan and stir well. Cook until heated through and stir in mussels.

3. Cover the pan and steam for 2 minutes until mussels open wide

4. Transfer mussels to a serving bowl and discard those that haven't opened.

5. Whisk butter into the sauce in the pan and remove from heat. Add parsley and green onions and stir.

Smoked Salmon and Artichoke Sauce

There are so many delicious ingredients in this recipe, it would be difficult to pinpoint just one that makes this dish amazing. Try serving this sauce over a bed of linguine with some freshly grated parmesan and garlic rolls.

Preparation Time: 15 minutes

Servings: 8

Ingredients:

- 1 ounce butter
- 1 ounce extra-virgin olive oil
- 16 ounces onions, coarsely chopped
- a pinch of salt and ground black pepper
- 4 coarsely chopped cloves garlic
- 14 ounce drained can of artichoke hearts, cut in quarters
- 8 ounces white wine
- 8 ounces chicken broth
- 1 ounce lemon juice
- 1/3 ounce lemon zest
- 1/4 teaspoon red pepper flakes
- 12 ounces chopped smoked salmon
- 8 ounces heavy whipping cream
- 4 ounces Parmesan cheese, grated

Directions:

1. Heat butter and oil in a large frying pan on medium heat.

2. Add onion to the butter and oil and stir for 5 minutes until translucent.

3. Stir in garlic and cook for 1 minute until fragrant.

4. Reduce the heat to medium low. Then add the wine, artichoke hearts, broth, lemon juice, pepper flakes and zest. Simmer for 10 minutes until liquid is reduced and sauce is thickened.

5. Stir in salmon, cream, parmesan, salt and pepper to the sauce and simmer for 5 minutes until thickened.

Sour Cream and Caviar Sauce

This sauce is comparable to any gourmet sauce you would find in a fine-dining seafood restaurant. Try serving this delectable dish with some fresh dill as garnish.

Preparation Time: 10 minutes

Servings: 8

Ingredients:

- 8 ounces sour cream
- 8 ounces creme fraiche
- 4 ounces mayonnaise
- 2 ounces fresh dill, chopped
- a pinch white pepper
- 3 1/2 ounces red lumpfish caviar

Directions:

1. Combine all ingredients together in a large bowl except for caviar. Gently stir in caviar and chill for 1 hour before serving

Lobster Sauce

Serve this creamy sauce over some linguine with a splash of sherry on top to enhance the taste. This tastes amazing when served with some fresh dinner rolls for dipping.

Preparation Time:30 minutes

Servings:6

Ingredients:

- 4 ounces butter
- 14 ounces diced lobster meat
- 1 medium diced onion
- 2 large diced stalks celery
- 2 peeled carrots, chopped
- 1 teaspoon fresh thyme, minced
- 1/8 teaspoon fresh parsley, chopped
- 1 teaspoon whole black peppercorns
- 1/8 teaspoon seasoned salt
- 1 bay leaf
- 1/8 teaspoon lemon juice
- 2 ounces all-purpose flour
- 1 ounce tomato paste
- 4 ounces cream sherry
- 32 ounces heavy cream
- 1/2 teaspoon salt and pepper

Directions:

1. Melt butter in a stockpot on medium heat. Add lobster, onion, celery, thyme, carrot, parsley, peppercorn, seasoning, bay leaf and freshly squeezed lemon juice in the pot with the butter and stir well. Cook for 10 minutes, stirring constantly until vegetables start to soften.

2. Add flour and tomato paste and stir constantly for 5 minutes.

3. Pour cream sherry into the mixture and cook for 2 minutes to burn off the alcohol.

4. Add heavy cream and bring sauce to a simmer, but do not boil. Reduce heat to low and cook for 15 minutes until the sauce is thick enough to cover the back of the spoon

5. Strain sauce through a mesh strainer into a large bowl and discard solid food left over.

6. Season with salt and pepper and serve

Lobster and Tomato Sauce

Instead of removing the lobster meat from the shell you can also keep half of the tails intact and serve over a bed of noodles. The sauce will still be meaty and your presentation will be stunning.

Preparation Time:20 minutes

Servings:6

Ingredients:

- 2 ounces olive oil
- 1 chopped onion
- 1 small crushed garlic clove
- 1/2 ounce fresh parsley, chopped
- 36 ounces thawed lobster tails
- 28 ounces canned crushed tomatoes
- 8 ounces tomato sauce
- 1 ½ ounces fresh basil, chopped
- a pinch of salt and ground black pepper

Directions:

1. Heat oil in a large pot on medium heat

2. Sauté onion and garlic in the oil for 8 minutes until browned lightly

3. Add parsley and lobster to the mixture in the pot and cook for 15 minutes until the shell turns a bright red

4. Stir in the remaining ingredients, reduce heat to low and simmer for 1 hour. Stir frequently

5. Remove lobster from the sauce and then remove the lobster meat from the shell. Add meat to the sauce and stir well before serving.

Cajun Shrimp Alfredo

Here is another Cajun-inspired seafood sauce recipe that will have your taste buds singing. I like to experiment with the Cajun seasoning and add more if I want to kick up the spice.

Preparation Time: 20 minutes

Servings: 6

Ingredients:

- 8 ounces diced andouille sausage
- 1/4 diced onion
- 2 ounces celery, diced
- 2 ounces red bell pepper, diced
- 1/3 ounce Cajun seasoning
- 1/4 teaspoon sage, dried
- 16 ounces peeled raw shrimp, deveined
- 14 ounces milk
- 1.6 ounce package dry Alfredo sauce mix
- 1/2 ounce butter
- 4 ounces Parmesan cheese, freshly grated
- 1/3 ounce minced garlic, divided

Directions:

1. In a large frying pan, mix andouille sausage, onion, celery, bell pepper, Cajun seasoning, and sage.

2. Cook for 10 minutes, stirring constantly until sausage is browned evenly and fully cooked

3. Stir shrimp into the mixture and cook for 5 minutes until bright pink. Remove frying pan from heat.

4. In another pan, whisk milk, Alfredo mix and butter together and bring to a boil.

5. Reduce heat to low and let sauce simmer for 2 minutes until thickened

6. Add parmesan cheese and garlic to the sauce and stir until cheese melts.

7. Stir in shrimp and sausage mixture from the pan until well combined and serve

Lobster Scampi

Lobster is one of my favorite seafood dishes to serve with pasta sauce because I find the taste irresistible. I usually use seasoned bread crumbs for this recipe or make my own.

Preparation Time:20 minutes

Servings:6

Ingredients:

- 6 ounces butter
- 3/4 ounce garlic, minced
- 24 ounces chopped cooked lobster meat
- 4 ounces white wine
- 1 teaspoon lemon juice
- 2 ounces Parmesan cheese, grated
- 4 ounces bread crumbs

Directions:

1. Melt butter in a frying pan on medium heat. Sauté garlic in the butter and cook for 5 minutes until fragrant.

2. Stir in lobster and cook for 10 minutes until heated through.

3. Add wine and lemon juice and bring mixture to a boil.

4. Stir in parmesan cheese and cook for 2 minutes until melted.

5. Slowly add bread crumbs 1 ounce at a time and bring the mixture to a boil after each addition.

Tuna Tomato Pasta Sauce II

I like serving this sauce with rigatoni noodles and plenty of parmesan sauce. I recommend a lovely fruity wine to cut the saltiness of the tuna.

Preparation Time:5 minutes

Servings:2

Ingredients:

- 1 ounce olive oil
- 1 small diced chile pepper
- 1 minced clove garlic
- 9 ounces canned tuna, drained
- 1 ½ ounces tomato paste
- 1/2 ounce white sugar
- 1 teaspoon salt
- 1 teaspoon black pepper, ground
- 22 ounces canned tomatoes, diced

Directions:

1.Heat oil in a large frying pan on medium heat and sauté chile pepper and garlic in the oil for 1 minute until browned lightly

2.Stir in tuna, paste, sugar, salt and pepper and cook for 5 minutes.

3.Add diced tomatoes and bring mixture to a simmer for 10 minutes.

Creamy Crab Sauce

My favorite pasta to serve with this sauce is pumpkin filled ravioli. Try pouring this sauce into a large serving bowl and then topping with tender cooked ravioli.

Preparation Time:5 minutes

Servings:4

Ingredients:

- 1 ounce butter
- 6 ounce can crabmeat
- 1/3 ounce dried thyme, crushed
- 16 ounces light cream
- 2 ounces Parmesan cheese, shredded
- a pinch of salt and ground white pepper

Directions:

1. Melt butter in a large pot on medium heat

2. Stir in crabmeat and thyme and cook for 2 minutes until fragrant

3. Pour cream into the mixture, increase the heat to medium high and cook for 5 minutes until cream steams.

4. Reduce heat to medium low and add parmesan. Stir for 2 minutes until cheese melts.

Seafood Pasta Sauce

Try this seafood pasta sauce tossed with linguine and sour cream. The taste is creamy and delicious especially with some fresh crusty bread rolls and a lovely glass of white wine.

Preparation Time: 20 minutes

Servings: 4

Ingredients:

- 2 ounces onion, chopped
- 2 crushed garlic cloves
- 1 teaspoon butter
- 1 teaspoon olive oil
- 8 ounces shrimp
- 8 ounces scallops
- 6 ½ ounces canned clams, with liquid
- 12 ounces chicken broth
- 1 teaspoon basil
- 1 ounce parsley
- 1/2 teaspoon paprika
- 1/4 teaspoon salt
- 1/4 teaspoon pepper
- 1/2 teaspoon Emeril's Original Essence

Directions:

1. Heat butter and oil in a large frying pan. Sauté onions and garlic in the pan for 5 minutes until onions are translucent and garlic is fragrant

2. Stir in shrimps and scallops and cook for 5 minutes.

3. Stir in the rest of the ingredients and bring the mixture to a simmer. Cook for 5 minutes.

4. Dissolve 1 ounce of cornstarch in 1 ½ ounces of water then add to the sauce to thicken.

Seafood Pasta in Lemon Butter Sauce

It is best to make this sauce while the pasta is cooking because it tastes amazing just fresh from the pot. Serve this with a glass of the same wine you use for cooking to complement the flavor.

Preparation Time:20 minutes

Servings:4

Ingredients:

- 1 medium chopped onion
- 4 ounces butter
- 2 ½ ounces olive oil
- 16 ounces peeled raw shrimp, deveined
- 8 ounces small raw scallops, cut in half
- 1 ounce lemon zest, minced
- 2 ounces lemon juice
- 2 ounces white wine
- A pinch of salt and pepper
- 2 ounces pine nuts, toasted
- Grated Romano to taste

Directions:

1. Heat butter and oil in a large pot on medium heat. Sauté onions in the butter and oil until translucent.

2. Stir in shrimp and scallops and cook for 5-10 minutes until shrimp just starts to turn bright pink.

3. Stir in lemon zest and juice, wine, salt and pepper until well combined and cook for 2 minutes until mixture is bubbly and shrimp is completely pink.

4. Serve sauce over your favorite pasta and top with parmesan and roasted pine nuts

Tomato Butter Sauce for Seafood

Try this delicious sauce with fettucine noodles and a glass of fruity white wine. Try buying the seafood mix from a fish market for the freshest taste.

Preparation Time:20 minutes

Servings:4

Ingredients:

- 8 ounces frozen seafood mix
- 4 minced cloves garlic
- 28 ounces canned whole peeled tomatoes
- 1/4 teaspoon red pepper flakes
- 1/2 teaspoon
- Fresh parsley for garnish

Directions:

1. Melt 1 ounce of butter in a large frying pan on medium heat   ·

2. Add seafood mix to the butter and stir and cook for 5 minutes until shrimp have turned a bright pink. Don't overcook the shrimp because they can get tough. Remove seafood to a large bowl and set aside.

3. In the same frying pan, melt 1 ounce of butter on medium heat. Sauté garlic in the butter and any drippings from the seafood for 2 minutes until fragrant.

4. Pour in can of tomatoes with juice and ¼ teaspoon of pepper flakes. Break the tomatoes into pieces as they cook.

5. Bring mixture to a simmer then reduce heat to medium low. Cook for 30 minutes continuing to break the tomatoes into small pieces. Stir mixture often. Add ½ teaspoon of salt to the sauce.

6. Pour seafood back into the pan and stir until heated through. Toss in your pasta and garnish with parsley.

Mushroom Cream Sauce

Serve this creamy mushroom sauce with some rotini noodles and crunchy sliced of garlic bread. I love the taste of the plump and juicy mushrooms in this delectable dish.

Preparation Time:20 minutes

Servings:4

Ingredients:

- 3 ounces butter
- 1 small garlic clove, halved
- 16 ounces fresh mushrooms, sliced
- 32 ounces bay scallops, cleaned
- 16 ounces peeled shrimp, deveined
- 12 ounces whipping cream
- 6 ounces Parmesan cheese, grated
- A pinch of kosher salt
- A pinch of ground black pepper

Directions

1. Melt butter in a large frying pan on medium heat. Sauté garlic in the butter until fragrant then add the sliced mushrooms. Cook for 5-10 minutes until browned and tender. Remove pieces of garlic from the pan.

2. Add scallops and shrimp to the pan and sauté with the mushrooms for 6 minutes until shrimp is bright pink. Don't overcook or the seafood will get tough.

3. Cook your pasta and toss with cream and parmesan.

4. In a large bowl, combine pasta noodles and mushroom sauce. Toss to combine, season with salt and pepper and garnish with parsley before serving.

20 Minute Seafood Pasta

This pasta sauce is quick and easy to make and enjoyable to devour! Try serving this with some spaghetti and lemon zest.

Preparation Time:20 minutes

Servings:4

Ingredients:

- ½ ounce olive oil
- 1 chopped onion
- 1 chopped clove garlic
- 1 teaspoon paprika
- 14 ounce can chopped tomatoes
- 33 ¾ ounces chicken stock
- 10 ½ ounces broken spaghetti
- 8 ½ ounces thawed frozen seafood mix
- Chopped parsley leaves for garnish
- 1 lemon cut in wedges

Directions

1. Heat oil in a large frying pan and sauté onion and garlic in the oil for 5 minutes until tender and fragrant.

2. Stir in paprika, chicken stock and tomatoes. Bring to a boil.

3. Reduce heat to a simmer, add spaghetti and cook for about 7 minutes until spaghetti is al dente

4. Add seafood mix to the pan and cook for 3 minutes, stirring constantly until pasta is cooked through.

5. Serve with parsley and lemon wedges

Linguine with Seafood Sauce

The tender linguine will melt in the mouth when devoured with this seafood sauce. This dish is chock full of delicacies that will have you reaching for seconds.

Preparation Time:20 minutes

Servings:4

Ingredients:

- 56 ounces peeled Italian plum tomatoes
- 1 ounce extra-virgin olive oil
- 2 large smashed garlic cloves
- 16 ounces clam juice
- 2 large thyme sprigs
- 4 large basil leaves
- A pinch of sugar
- A pinch of salt and ground pepper
- 32 ounces cleaned baby squid, sliced across in ½" rings. Cut large tentacles in half
- 24 ounces thin linguine
- 32 ounces clean and debearded mussels
- 36 scrubbed cockles, soaked in cold water for 2 hours and drained
- 16 ounces peeled and deveined medium shrimp
- Crushed red pepper to taste

Directions

1.Place plum tomatoes in a blender and puree until smooth. Press tomatoes

2.Heat oil in a large heavy-bottomed pot on medium high heat. Sauté garlic in the oil for 30 seconds until fragrant.

3.Stir in tomato mixture from the blender, clam juice, thyme, basil, sugar, salt and pepper. Bring to a boil.

4.Reduce heat to medium low and cook for 45 minutes until 1/3 of the liquid has been reduced.

5.Reduce heat to low and add squid. Cook for 45 minutes more until squid is tender.

Red Seafood Sauce

The plump and juicy shrimp taste amazing when mixed in with this creamy sauce. I like to serve this over a bed of linguine with a chilled glass of white wine.

Preparation Time:45 minutes

Servings:6

Ingredients:

- 28 ounces can of crushed tomatoes
- 8 ounces chopped onion
- 4 minced garlic cloves
- 1 minced shallot
- 1 ½ ounces olive oil
- 1/2 teaspoon red pepper flakes
- 1 teaspoon salt
- 1 teaspoon ground black pepper
- 8 ounces dry white wine
- 8 ounces clam juice
- ½ ounce minced thyme
- 1 minced fresh bay leaf
- 16 ounces peeled and deveined shrimp

Directions

1. Heat oil in a saucepan on medium heat. Sauté onion in the oil for 10 minutes until translucent

2. Stir in garlic and shallot for 5 minutes until fragrant.

3. Add bell pepper, salt and pepper to the mixture in the pan and cook for 1-2 minutes more.

4. Stir in the remaining ingredients except for the shrimp, reduce heat to low and cook for 20-30 minutes.

5. Just before serving, add shrimp to the sauce and cook until bright pink.

6. Serve with pasta

Seafood Arrabiatta Sauce

Try serving this delicious arrabiatta sauce with some linguine and some crusty dinner rolls. It is best to prepare the sauce while the pasta is cooking so both are fresh and hot when you combine them.

Preparation Time:30 minutes

Servings:4

Ingredients:

- 1 ounces extra-virgin olive oil, divided
- 6 ounces bay scallops
- 6 ounces medium shrimp, peeled and deveined
- 8 ounces onion, chopped
- 1/2 teaspoon crushed red pepper
- 3 minced garlic cloves
- 1 ounce tomato paste
- 14 ½ ounce drained can petite-cut diced tomatoes
- 4 ounces clam juice
- 12 littleneck clams
- 12 scrubbed and debearded mussels
- 1 ounce fresh parsley, chopped
- ½ ounce fresh basil, thinly sliced

Directions

1.Heat ½ ounce of oil in a large frying pan on medium high heat.

2.Add scallops and shrimp to the oil and cook for 3 minutes until the shrimp are just starting to turn pink.

3.Remove scallops and shrimp from the pan and set aside. Cover to keep warm. Heat the rest of the oil in the same pan on medium high heat.

4.Add onion, bell pepper and garlic to the oil and cook for 2 minutes until tender. Stir in tomato paste and tomatoes and bring to a boil. Cook mixture for 2 minutes.

5.Pour in clam juice and cook for 1 minute. Add clams to the pan, cover and cook for 4 minutes.

6.Place mussels in the pan, cover again and cook for another 3 minutes until mussels and clams open.

7.Remove any unopened shells and discard.

8.Stir in scallops and shrimp and cook for 1-2 minutes until shrimp are bright pink and heated through.

9.Serve with your favorite pasta and garnish with basil.

Conclusion

When you love seafood and pasta then combining the two tastes is a natural thing to do for mealtime. The amazing tastes and textures of mussels, scallops, shrimp, clams and lobster found in these recipes will have your taste buds singing. Try these dishes with your favorite pasta like linguine, rigatoni or spaghetti and taste the difference a seafood sauce can make for your pasta meal.

Author's Afterthoughts

Thanks Ever So Much to Each of My Cherished Readers for Investing the Time to Read This Book!

I know you could have picked from many other books but you chose this one. So, big thanks for buying this book and reading all the way to the end.

If you enjoyed this book or received value from it, I'd like to ask you for a favor. Please take a few minutes to post an honest and heartfelt review on **Amazon.** Your support does make a difference and helps to benefit other people.

Thank you!

Carla Hale

About the Author

Carla Hale

I think of myself as a foodie. I like to eat, yes. I like to cook even more. I like to prepare meals for my family and friends, I feel like that's what I was born to do...

My name is Carla Hale and as may have suspected already, I am originally from Scotland. I am first and foremost a mother, a wife, but simultaneously over the years I became a proclaimed cook. I have shared my recipes with many and will continue to do so, as long as I can. I like different. I dress different, I love different, I speak different and I cook different. I like to think that I am different because I am more animated about what I do than most; I feel more and care more.

It served me right when cooking to sprinkle some tenderness, love, passion, in every dish I prepare. It does not matter if I am preparing a meal for strangers passing by my cooking booth at the flea market or if I am making my mother's favorite recipe. Each and every meal I prepare from scratch will contain a little bite of my life story and little part of my heart in it. People feel it, taste it and ask for more! Thank you for taking the time to get to know me and hopefully through my recipes you can learn a lot more about my influences and preferences. Who knows you might just find your own favorite within my repertoire! Enjoy!

Printed in Great Britain
by Amazon

49475400R00054